C000225482

About Demos

Demos is a greenhouse for new ideas which can improve the quality of our lives. As an independent think tank, we aim to create an open resource of knowledge and learning that operates beyond traditional party politics.

We connect researchers, thinkers and practitioners to an international network of people changing politics. Our ideas regularly influence government policy, but we also work with companies, NGOs, colleges and professional bodies.

Demos knowledge is organised around five themes, which combine to create new perspectives. The themes are democracy, learning, enterprise, quality of life and global change.

But we also understand that thinking by itself is not enough. Demos has helped to initiate a number of practical projects which are delivering real social benefit through the redesign of public services.

We bring together people from a wide range of backgrounds to cross-fertilise ideas and experience. By working with Demos, our partners develop a sharper insight into the way ideas shape society. For Demos, the process is as important as the final product.

www.demos.co.uk

First published in 2004
© Demos
Some rights reserved – see copyright licence for details

ISBN 1 84180 136 4
Typeset by Land & Unwin, Bugbrooke
Printed by HenDI Systems, London

For further information and
subscription details please contact:

Demos
Magdalen House
136 Tooley Street
London SE1 2TU

telephone: 0845 458 5949
email: hello@demos.co.uk
web: www.demos.co.uk

The Pro-Am Revolution

How enthusiasts are changing our society and economy

Charles Leadbeater
Paul Miller

DEMOS

Contents

Acknowledgements

Many people helped with the research and preparation of this report. We would like to thank David Abraham and Diane Charvet at Discovery, Alex Darlington at Orange and Nicholas Gilby at MORI, as well of course as all the Pro-Ams we interviewed in the course of the project. At Demos, Rachel McLachlan and James Wilsdon helped shape the project and Peter Macleod did invaluable and uphill work helping to gather statistics on Pro-Am activities. Helen McCarthy, Sophia Parker, Eddie Gibb and Paul Skidmore all provided helpful comments and Lisa Linklater saw the report through to publication. As always, however, all errors and omissions are our own.

Charles Leadbeater
Paul Miller
November 2004

For me work is the oddity. Work is a kind of compromise. I do work which is as close as possible to my passions to make working tolerable. But I feel most myself when I am doing this open source stuff. When I am doing this and give it my complete and full attention then everything else around me fades away and dissolves and I become completely focused.

Seb Potter, Pro-Am open source programmer

When I am working on a garden it's quite tough and demanding. I do a lot of research and thinking about it. But it does not feel like work. It never feels like a chore.

Dilip Lakhani, Pro-Am garden designer

... climbing says more about who I am than my job. Journalism is my trade but climbing is my passion.

Brendan Sheehan, Pro-Am rock climber

1. Pro-Am power

Rap music, the Jubilee Debt Campaign, the Linux open source software movement and *The Sims* computer game have all left their mark on the world in the last decade. Rap infects all popular culture. The Jubilee campaign led to billions of dollars of developing world debt being written off. Linux is one of the biggest challengers to Microsoft. *The Sims* is one of the most popular computer games ever. These developments have one thing in common: they were all driven by Pro-Ams, innovative, committed and networked amateurs working to professional standards. This emerging group, the Pro-Ams, could have a huge influence on the shape of society in the next two decades.

According to many commentators, the 1990s were a decade in which large corporations were rampant, their control over society virtually unchallenged.[1] Yet the rise of Pro-Ams suggests counter trends were at work as well.

Rap started as do-it-yourself music, among lower income black men from distressed urban neighbourhoods in the US, who used their lyrics to draw attention to their feelings of anger, frustration and violence. Most Rap was originally performed by artists in their own homes, with their own inexpensive equipment. It was distributed on handmade tapes, by local independent record labels. Yet within two decades urban black music has become the dominant force in global popular culture. It is not the only Pro-Am movement transforming popular music. Do-it-yourself file sharing, through Napster and its offspring, Kazaa and others, has created a peer-to-peer Pro-Am distribution system.

Linux, the computer operating system, started life in September 1991, when Linus Torvalds, then a pasty-looking computer student at Helsinki University in Finland, posted the source code for his new operating system on the internet and asked his fellow software enthusiasts to make criticisms, propose improvements, take it away and tamper with it. They responded in droves. Torvalds set off a process of mass, participatory innovation among thousands of Pro-Am software programmers. Many of them program software for a living but became involved in Linux in their spare time because the spirit of collaborative problem-solving appealed so strongly.

By 2004 about 20 million people around the world were using a version of Linux. There were 430 user communities in more than 72 countries and more than 120,000 registered Linux users, many of whom helped with its development.[2] Linux is just one of several internet-related innovations that have emerged from groups of Pro-Ams.[3] Half the websites on the internet depend on Pro-Am, open source Apache software. Most email uses sendmail, a program created by Pro-Ams. Usenet newsgroups are supported by the hacker-created INN program and the internet's plain language address system, eg www.demos.co.uk, depends on the Pro-Am-created BIND program. The personal computer started life in the Pro-Am Homebrew Computer Club.[4]

The Jubilee 2000 debt campaign, which changed the way we think about debt and international development, started life with one campaigner working in a shed near London's South Bank in the mid-1990s. By the year 2000 it had a petition with 24 million signatures, had spawned a network of 69 national campaigns and mobilised hundreds of thousands of people in protest in the UK. At least US$36 billion of developing world debt has been written off as a result. No mean achievement for a campaign that was largely organised by Pro-Am campaigners, and had little formal structure and few professional staff. The Jubilee Debt Campaign as it is now known, is just one outstanding example of the way that Pro-Am political campaigners are driving single issue, pressure group politics. The massive growth in non-governmental organisations around the world in the last decade is largely due to Pro-Am political campaigners. Pro-Ams are reshaping the way democracy works.[5]

Finally, take *The Sims* computer game. A *Sims* player can create their own family home on a computer and watch the inhabitants sleep, eat, argue, marry, make love, fight and die. Before the online version was shipped, the designers released tools that allowed players to create their own content for the game: furniture, accessories, even architectural styles for houses. Within a year of the game's initial release there were hundreds of independent content creators, more than 200 fan websites displaying more than half a million collectable items available to the game's millions of players. More than 90 per cent of the content in the *Sims* game is now created by a Pro-am sector of the *Sims* playing community. One estimate is that there are 30,000 Pro-Am modifications to the *Sims* game that can be downloaded from the internet. The *Sims* community is a distributed, bottom-up, self-organising body of Pro-Am knowledge, in which players are constantly training one another and innovating.[6] This is just one among many examples of how communities of Pro-Am gamers are helping to co-create the games they play.

Pro-Am power is not confined to the high-tech, developed world. It also works in some of the poorest communities. Many of the social and medical advances of the twentieth century – especially in health, social work, finance and education – have relied on providing people with access to professional expertise: teachers deliver education, doctors cure disease. Many of these advances have bypassed people in the developing world where professionals are scarce and expensive. Professionals create a distribution bottleneck. That is why many of the most imaginative social innovations in the developing world employ Pro-Am forms of organisation.

An outstanding example is Bangladesh's Grameen Bank founded in 1976 by Muhammad Yunnus, a Bangladeshi economics professor, to provide very poor people with access to microcredit to allow them to improve their houses and invest in businesses. Traditional banks, reliant on professional expertise, regarded poor people seeking small loans as unprofitable. Grameen built a different model, based on Pro-Am expertise. It employs a small body of professionals who train an army of barefoot bankers. Village committees administer most of Grameen's loans. This Pro-Am workforce makes it possible to administer millions of tiny loans cost-effectively. By 2003, Grameen had lent more than US$4 billion to about 2.8 million Bangladeshis, including 570,000 mortgages to build tin roofs for huts to keep people dry during the monsoons. Had Grameen relied on traditional, professional models of organisation it would only have reached a tiny proportion of the population.[7]

These five examples show that when Pro-Ams are networked together they can have a huge impact on politics and culture, economics and development. Pro-Ams can achieve things that until recently only large, professional organisations could achieve.

The twentieth century was shaped by the rise of professionals in most walks of life. From education, science and medicine, to banking, business and sports, formerly amateur activities became more organised, and knowledge and procedures were codified and regulated. As professionalism grew, often with hierarchical organisations and formal systems for accrediting knowledge, so amateurs came to be seen as second-rate. Amateurism came to be to a term of derision. Professionalism was a mark of seriousness and high standards.

But in the last two decades a new breed of amateur has emerged: the Pro-Am, amateurs who work to professional standards. These are not the gentlemanly amateurs of old – George Orwell's blimpocracy, the men in blazers who sustained amateur cricket and athletics clubs.[8] The Pro-Ams are knowledgeable, educated, committed and networked, by new technology. The twentieth century was shaped by large hierarchical organisations with professionals at the top. Pro-Ams are creating new, distributed organisational models that will be innovative, adaptive and low-cost. An outstanding example of how Pro-Ams are transforming a field is astronomy.

Pro-Am, open source astronomy

On the night of 23 February 1987, light reached Earth from a star that had exploded on the edge of the Tarantula nebula 168,000 years earlier. The supernova was enormous and was the first to be witnessed by the naked eye since 1604. In the Chilean Andes, Ian Shelton, an avid amateur astronomer who was on the verge of turning professional, took a photograph with a 10" telescope. Shelton went down in history as the man who discovered supernova 1987A.[9]

That night two other dedicated amateur astronomers were at work. Albert Jones, a veteran with more than half a million observations to his credit, had taken a good look at the Tarantula nebula earlier but had seen nothing unusual. Robert McNaught, another Pro-Am, photographed the explosion at 10.30 UT in Australia.[10]

Together these amateurs played a vital role in confirming a theory that explains what happens when a star explodes. Astrophysicists theorised that when a star explodes most of its energy is released as neutrinos, low-mass, subatomic particles which fly through planets as if they are not there. When a star explodes the neutrinos should exit at high speed and arrive on earth two hours before the light.

On the night of 23 February a large storm of neutrinos from Shelton's supernova was detected by labs in the US and Japan at 7.35 UT. According to the theory the first light should have arrived at 9.35 UT. Jones checked his meticulous records and confirmed that when he was looking at Tarantula at 9.30 UT he had not seen any sign of an explosion. That meant the neutrinos had already arrived yet the light had not, just as the theory predicted. When McNaught's photograph from Australia was taken at 10.30 UT, the light of the explosion was visible. A key theory explaining how the universe works had been confirmed thanks to amateurs in New Zealand and Australia, a former amateur turning professional in Chile and professional physicists in the US and Japan. These were the joint authors of the discovery made by a loosely connected Pro-Am team.

As Timothy Ferris points out in *Seeing in the Dark*, his history of modern amateur astronomy: 'If one were to choose a date at which astronomy shifted from the old days of solitary professionals at their telescopes to a worldwide web linking professionals and amateurs ... a good candidate would be the night of February 23rd 1987.'[11] Astronomy is fast becoming a science driven by a vast open source Pro-Am movement working alongside a much smaller body of professional astronomers and astrophysicists.

Amateurs laid the foundations for modern astronomy. Copernicus, who moved the sun to the centre of the universe, was only a sometime astronomer. Johannes Kepler, who discovered that the planets orbit in ellipses made most of his money from horoscopes. But by the twentieth century the pendulum had swung decisively in favour of the professionals, for one simple reason: scale. Professional astronomers had access to huge telescopes, like Jodrell Bank in the UK or the Mt Wilson Observatory near Pasedena where Howard Shapley established that the Sun is located to one edge of our galaxy and Edwin Hubble determined that the galaxies are being carried away from one another into cosmic space. Professionals probed the outer depths of space, home to the most troubling scientific mysteries. Amateurs, with their puny telescopes, concentrated on closer, well known and brighter objects.

But in the last two decades three linked innovations have turned astronomy into an open source, Pro-Am activity. A disruptive innovation made powerful telescopes cheap enough for the average astronomer. John Dobson, a one-time monk and lifelong star gazer designed a crude but powerful telescope using discarded and secondhand materials. Dobson's philosophy was pure open source: 'To me it's not so much how big your telescope is, or how accurately your optics are, or how beautiful the pictures you can take with it; it's how many people in this vast world less privileged than you have had a chance to see through your telescope and understand this universe.'[12] Dobson refused to profit from his invention, which he never patented. Soon many companies were making Dobsonian telescopes. Observers armed with a mighty Dobsonian could invade the deep space that had previously been the preserve of the professionals. Then the CCD (charged coupled device) came along, a highly light-sensitive chip, which could record very faint starlight much faster than a photograph. Amateurs who attached a CCD to a large Dobsonian found themselves with light-gathering capacity to match the giant 200" telescopes professionals had used 20 years earlier.

An open source catchphrase is that 'many eyes make bugs shallow': the more programmers looking at a problem, the easier it is to solve. The same is true of some aspects of astronomy. Thanks to Dobsonian telescopes with CCD sensors the Earth acquired hundreds of thousands of new eyes, probing deep space, recording events that would have gone unnoticed by the much smaller body of professionals. This distributed capacity for exploration and observation was vastly enhanced by the internet. Before the internet, an amateur who had discovered something new would send a telegram to the Harvard College Observatory. Once the professionals had checked out the claim, they would mail a postcard to observatories around the world. These days if amateurs finds something interesting they can email the image to friends, colleagues and professionals within minutes. Crude Dobsonian telescopes armed with CCDs have given the Earth thousands of new eyes, says Ferris; the net provided it with new optic nerves.

In the 1990s, thanks to these three innovations, new forms of organisation started to emerge. Astronomy used to be done in 'big science' research institutes. Now it is also done in Pro-Am collaboratives. Many amateurs continued to work on their own and many professionals were still ensconced in their academic institutions. But global research networks sprang up, linking professionals and amateurs with shared interests in flare stars, comets and asteroids. Pro-Am astronomers tracked the weather on Jupiter and craters on Mars as accurately as professionals. They detected echoes from colliding galaxies and more than one million Pro-Am astronomers in more than 200 countries are contributing their computers' idle time to analyse data that might be evidence of extraterrestrial life.

There are limits to what Pro-Ams can achieve. Amateurs do not produce new theories of astrophysics. Sometimes amateurs do not know how to make sense of the data they have acquired. Yet the future of astronomy, and perhaps after it biology and other sciences, will be as a Pro-Am activity, with dedicated amateurs and professionals working in tandem, motivated by the same sense of excitement about exploring the universe. As John Lankford, a historian of science put it in *Sky & Telescope* magazine, the bible of US amateur astronomers: 'There will always remain a division of labour between professionals and amateurs. But it may be more difficult to tell the two groups apart in future.'[13]

Some professionals will seek to defend their endangered monopoly. The more enlightened will understand that knowledge is widely distributed, not controlled in a few ivory towers. The most powerful organisations will combine the know-how of professionals and amateurs to solve complex problems. That is true in astronomy, software development and online games. It should be the path that our health, education and welfare systems follow as well.

It was professional in the sense that I was paid, but the rates were well below Equity rates. I was running a small management consulting business at the time and I would treat going on tour like going off to do a project. Most actors have day jobs. But they work in bars or restaurants. I had a day job but it was a serious management job. For me taking time to act was an opportunity to lose money. I called myself a professional actor but in reality it was an expensive way to lose money.

Alison Maguire, Pro-Am actor

I didn't just want to do the kind of self-build where you hire someone else to do it for you. I wanted to get down and get muddy doing the stuff I love. . . . Even if I do say so myself, I'm somewhat above average in the DIY stakes. I can do things as well as the professionals, it just takes me a bit longer.

Ben Tuxworth, Pro-Am house builder

I don't want to take a big risk and shift over completely. I could become a professional, full-time garden designer if it took off, but I'd prefer to see how it builds up slowly. I feel I am learning new skills the whole time and coming up against new challenges. Every project is different and poses new challenges. I feel stretched by this in a way I do not feel at work. It's a very creative feeling. You know when something is right.

Dilip Lakhani, Pro-Am garden designer

2. The Pro-Am idea

James Stewart describes himself, self-deprecatingly, as a 'wannabe tennis pro'. Tennis dominates his life. He started playing on public courts in Hackney when he was nine and at the age of ten played his first competitive game. During his teens James's tennis playing became more competitive, but when most of his tennis peers left school at 16 to become professionals, James went on to do A levels and from there to Loughborough University on a tennis scholarship. After he left university he had some job interviews with banks but instead he took a job coaching at a north London tennis centre. One of his adult pupils suggested he should start playing competitively again. To play professionally, a player has to get a 'rating' in a world-wide rating system which ranks players from 10 up to 1, the best.

Good amateurs often have ratings in the 10–5 range. Only those with a ranking less than 4 can get into national British tournaments. Above that are Futures tournaments for emerging players, Challenger tournaments for professional players just below the top of the game and then finally the ATP tour with the likes of Agassi, Henman and Federer. James started in the amateur foothills of this worldwide system with tournaments played in the evenings. At the age of 26, James's life is dedicated to improving his national rating, which now stands at close to 2 and acquiring an elusive world ranking point that will get him into bigger tournaments.

On an average day he is up at 6.30am and plays tennis against someone of his standard for two hours from 8am. After a rest they play for a further two hours, to 1pm. He has a big lunch and a nap before going to the gym. In the afternoon and early evening he coaches tennis, mainly to kids. That is his only source of regular income. After another big meal in the evening he sits down in front of the television to watch tennis. He reads two tennis magazines a month and watches anything up to three hours of tennis a night on satellite television. James also uses the web and his mobile phone to organise his activities. 'I could not survive without my mobile phone. I am away a lot at tournaments so it allows me to keep in touch, especially with people I am coaching. I can only sustain playing in tournaments by coaching so keeping in touch with clients is vital.' He coaches for perhaps 20 hours a week and most of the appointments are organised via his mobile.

James frequently visits a specialist, non-profit website, Steve G Tennis, which gathers results from Futures tournaments from around the world, including the qualifying rounds. Even specialist tennis magazines do not report these results. The Tennis One site provides digital footage, from several angles, of all the shots played by all the leading main players. If you want to see Andre Agassi's sliced cross-court backhand from three angles, in slow motion, you can. James books all his cheap hotels and bed and breakfast accommodation for tournaments via the internet.

Sustaining his Pro-Am lifestyle is a costly business. He has three rackets that need restringing once a week. A decent stringing machine costs about £1,500. A set of tennis balls, which last about an hour's intense practice, costs £6. He needs new tennis shoes every three weeks and a constant supply of clothing. The main expense is going to the tournaments, which generally take place with no spectators in anonymous sports centres around the country from Plymouth to Cardiff, Hull to North Wales. At the peak of the season James aims to be playing three tournaments a month, at a cost of about £200 per tournament. And often it's a long and fruitless journey.

It's tough driving all the way to somewhere like Hull, checking
into a bed and breakfast on your own, and getting yourself ready

*only to be knocked out in the first round and then having to
drive yourself all the way back to London. I cannot afford a
coach. I have to motivate myself and pick myself up. But if I
didn't think that at some point I could turn professional I would
not do it.*

James Stewart is a Pro-Am: he bridges the professional and amateur
divide. He is not a professional tennis player, even though he spends
all his time playing tennis and earns his living from coaching. He
plays tennis because he loves it; he's not in it for the money. Tennis is
vital to his sense of identity. Yet James is not an amateur: he pursues
his tennis with the dedication of a professional. He can trace a career
in the sport, through which he has learned skills and earned rankings.
He judges himself by professional standards.

There are going to be more Pro-Ams in more walks of life and they
are set to have a significant influence on society: socially, politically
and economically.

A Pro-Am pursues an activity as an amateur, mainly for the love of
it, but sets a professional standard. Pro-Ams are unlikely to earn more
than a small portion of their income from their pastime but they
pursue it with the dedication and commitment associated with a
professional. For Pro-Ams, leisure is not passive consumerism but
active and participatory; it involves the deployment of publicly
accredited knowledge and skills, often built up over a long career,
which has involved sacrifices and frustrations.

Pro-Ams demand we rethink many of the categories through
which we divide up our lives.[14] Pro-Ams are a new social hybrid.
Their activities are not adequately captured by the traditional
definitions of work and leisure, professional and amateur, consumption and production. We use a variety of terms – many
derogatory, none satisfactory – to describe what people do with their
serious leisure time: nerds, geeks, anoraks, enthusiasts, hackers, men
in their sheds. Our research suggests the best way to cover all the
activities covered by these terms is to call the people involved Pro-
Ams.

Working at leisure

Most Pro-Am activities take place outside normal working hours in the evenings, holidays and at weekends. So it makes sense to define these activities as 'non-work' and so as leisure. Leisure is usually defined as a form of relaxation that allows people to recuperate from work.

Yet Pro-Am leisure is a very serious activity involving training, rehearsal, competition and grading, and so also frustration, sacrifice, anxiety and tenacity. Pro-Ams report being absorbed in their activities, which yield intense experiences of creativity and self-expression. Pro-Am activities seem to provide people with psychic recuperation from – and an alternative to – work that is often seen as drudgery. Leisure is often regarded as a zone of freedom and spontaneity, which contrasts with the necessity of work. Yet much Pro-Am activity is also characterised by a sense of obligation and necessity. Pro-Ams talk of their activities as compulsions.

Work in organisations is defined by having to adhere to work schedules laid down by others. Many Pro-Ams engage in scheduled activities: practice and rehearsal sessions, for example. Yet the sense of control they feel over their time is vital to the pleasure they get. Pro-Ams can opt out if they wish, take a break. It's not compulsory.

Pro-Am activities highlight the need to distinguish more carefully between serious and casual, active and passive, forms of leisure.

As Rebecca Abrams puts it in *The Playful Self*:

> *Play gives colour to the monochrome of daily existence. It is the salt to the meat of our everyday lives. A world of work without play is a recipe for tense, stressed, bored people, who are not only not working to the best of their ability, but not living to the best of their ability.*[15]

Consumption as production

Pro-Ams spend a large share of their disposable income supporting their pastimes, whether through travel, equipment or entering tournaments. Often they spend to become producers of services. Pro-Am actors who use their holidays to put on touring productions are investing their money to produce theatre. Computer programmers who are part of the open source movement buy computers, not just to play games, but to write better software for others to use. Pro-Am musicians and photographers want to use their instruments and cameras to produce work that other people want to hear and see.

Pro-Ams create a sense of identity for themselves through consumption. Pro-Ams build up forms of 'cultural capital' that they can deploy in their hobbies. This 'cultural capital' is made up of skills and knowledge, of the norms and practices, of disciplines and subcultures, which then allows them to become part of that group or pastime.

Amateurs with professional standards

Pro-Ams are not professionals. They do not see themselves that way. They do not earn more than 50 per cent of their income from their Pro-Am activities. They might be aspiring proto-professionals, semi-professionals or former-professionals, but they would not be regarded as full professionals.

Yet to call Pro-Ams amateurs is also misleading. For many people 'amateur' is a term of derision: second-rate, not up to scratch, below par. Pro-Ams want to be judged by professional standards.

Many of the defining features of professionalism also apply to Pro-Ams: they have a strong sense of vocation; they use recognised public standards to assess performance and formally validate skills; they form self-regulating communities, which provide people with a sense of community and belonging; they produce non-commodity products and services; they are well versed in a body of knowledge and skill, which carries with it a sense of tradition and identity. Pro-Ams often have second, shadow or parallel careers that they turn to once their formal and public career comes to an end.

Professionals are distinguished by the nature of their knowledge. Professionals are more likely to understand the theory behind good practice, while Pro-Ams might have strong know-how and technique.

The stronger theoretical knowledge base of the professionals should allow them more scope for analysis and generalisation. It's easy to be a Pro-Am stargazer, but difficult to be a Pro-Am theoretical physicist. The relationship between amateurs and professionals is becoming more fluid and dynamic. It is not a zero-sum game. Professionals and Pro-Ams can grow together.

Pro-Ams work at their leisure, regard consumption as a productive activity and set professional standards to judge their amateur efforts.

Pro-Ams force us to distinguish 'serious' leisure – which requires regular commitment, skills and effort – from 'casual' leisure, which is more occasional and opportunistic. 'Active' leisure, which requires the physical or mental engagement of participants should be distinguished from more 'passive' forms of leisure, in which consumers are recipients of entertainment. Leisure is not homogenous: a lump of time left over after work. People engage in leisure activities of quite different intensities.

Pro-Ams demand that we see professionals and amateurs along a continuum (see diagram below). Fully-fledged professionals are at one end of the spectrum, but close by we have pre-professionals (apprentices and trainees), semi-professionals (who earn a significant part of their income from an activity) and post-professionals (former professionals who continue to perform or play once their professional career is over.) These latter three groups of 'quasi' professionals are Pro-Ams.

		Pro-Ams		
Devotees, fans, dabblers and spectators	Skilled amateurs	Serious and committed amateurs	Quasi-professionals	Fully-fledged professionals

These quasi-professionals often overlap with people who are serious and committed amateurs, who take part in public competitions, performances and displays. Skilled amateurs can be distinguished from amateurs who do not compete or perform. The continuum then stretches back to devotees, fans, dabblers and spectators.

As you move from left to right along this continuum, the amount of knowledge, time and money earned from an activity (and invested in it) goes up. Pro-Ams operate in a range somewhere around the third-quarter of the line.

There are lots of people in the climbing community who gather in places like this. Many of them have interim jobs, in computer programming or the creative industries, which allow them time to go off and climb for extended periods. There are very few people who can be full-time climbers, even full-time climbing instructors. There just isn't enough money in it to sustain a professional. The standards are not set by professionals but by the leading practitioners who tend to be committed amateurs: they set the standards technically, ethically, socially.

Brendan Sheehan, Pro-Am mountain climber

We set high standards which we expect people to match. To be accepted into the company you have to go through an audition in front of a panel of three and perform two contrasting pieces, to show that you have technique and that you are castable. The process is just like that in the professional theatre.

Alison Maguire, Pro-Am actor

You do make quite a lot of friends through St John's. I was down at the London Marathon a couple of weeks ago and I kept on bumping into people who I know through St John's. It was a lovely feeling.

Tendayi Bloom, Pro-Am paramedic

3. Measuring the Pro-Am sector

Getting a fix on the scale of Pro-Am activity is tricky not least because it is a hybrid category not recognised by standard research techniques. As a result, estimates of Pro-Am activity rely on proxies.

British figures suggest that club membership and community participation is holding up, especially in volunteering, in contrast to the decline charted by Robert Putnam in *Bowling Alone*.[16] While some traditional forms of association have dwindled – membership of the Women's Institute fell from 442,000 in 1972, to 240,000 30 years later for example – new networks have risen. Membership of environmental groups rose over the same period from 750,000 to close to 6 million. According to the British Social Attitudes Survey for 1998, about 21 per cent of people were members of community groups and 26 per cent were members of sports and cultural groups. The 2002 European Social Survey found these levels of participation in what might be the basis for Pro-Am activities (see Table 1).

The Electoral Commission's December 2003 Audit of Political Engagement found levels of participation in Pro-Am related activities as shown in Table 2.

The following snapshots provide some evidence of the wide spread of Pro-Am activity.

About 23 million adults a year undertake some form of volunteering, contributing close to 90 million hours a week. Volunteering has almost doubled in the last decade. There are

Table 1. Per cent reporting having participated in following activities in past 12 months

Activities	% Women	% Men
Member of political party	2	4
Church group	18	10
Environmental group	6	6
Humanitarian group	3	4
Educational group	6	7
Hobby groups	14	19
Social club	13	19
Consumer group	28	35
Sports club	20	33

Source: 2002 European Social Survey

Table 2. Percentage reporting having participated in following activities in the past 2–3 years

Activities	% Women	% Men
Political campaigning	3	3
Fundraising	17	25
Organising charity events	14	18
Voluntary work	21	24
Served as an club officer	9	6

Source: Electoral Commission, Audit of Political Engagement, December 2003

perhaps 5.7 million unpaid carers, who provide services worth £30 billion a year. The government's Millennium Volunteers scheme aimed to recruit 100,000 young volunteers by 2004 and the Experience Corps for volunteers over the age of 50 aimed to recruit 250,000.

Among important volunteer Pro-Am organisations are the Samaritans with 18,000 Pro-Am volunteer counsellors who devote 2.7 million hours a year; the Women's Royal Voluntary Service, which has

95,000 volunteers who deliver more than nine million Meals on Wheels a year; Neighbourhood Watch, which covers 27 per cent of households; and Victim Support, which has almost 15,000 volunteer Pro-Am counsellors. About 95 per cent of criminal cases are dealt with by the country's 26,000 Pro-Am magistrates.

The St John Ambulance is run by about 43,000 Pro-Ams and trains more than half a million people a year in first aid. The Surf Life Saving Association has 4,000 Pro-Am members who serve on British beaches.

In science there are estimated to be at least 4,500 independent archaeologists, not counting men who go out with metal detectors at weekends. The Natural History Museum estimates that 100,000 amateurs are actively involved in nature conservation, through a myriad of specialist societies and clubs. More than one million people are members of wildlife groups in the UK.

Family history is one of the fastest growing activities on the internet and local history rooms in public libraries are overflowing with members of the do-it-yourself history movement. The Family Record Centre in London estimates there are 387,000 active members of family history societies in the UK. A recent survey of more than 6,000 people conducted for the Arts Council found that 14 per cent regularly were engaged in painting or drawing, a further 14 per cent had craft hobbies and 9 per cent played musical instruments. In the North East, to take one example, about 6,000 clubs and voluntary associations organise cultural activities. About 138,000 people are members of the UK's Making Music societies, which put on more than 8,000 Pro-Am concerts a year, 550 workshops and 180 educational events. About 9 per cent of people play a musical instrument for pleasure, 2 per cent play to an audience at least once a year and 5 per cent sing to an audience at least once a year, according to Arts Council research.

Research commissioned by the Crafts Council found that 2 per cent of adults take part in Pro-Am drama, 4 per cent ballroom dancing, 2 per cent sing in choirs, 6 per cent write poetry or short stories, 8 per cent paint or draw, 19 per cent undertake photography,

14 per cent undertake some kind of creative work involving wood or metal and 11 per cent engage in needlework and textiles. According to the Pew Institute in America perhaps 7 per cent of internet users are active bloggers, using the internet to publish their arguments, thoughts and diaries.[17]

According to a study commissioned by the Central Council for Physical Recreation published in 2001, there are almost 5.8 million members of more than 110,000 amateur sports clubs in the UK.[18] These clubs are organised by perhaps 1.5 million Pro-Ams who contribute work equivalent to 720,000 full-time employees. A 2002 study published by Sports England found there were 431,000 volunteer organisers in football, 238,000 in cricket, 135,000 in bowls clubs, 82,000 in rugby union, 61,000 in swimming and motor racing and 30,000 in athletics. There are more than two million active gardeners in the UK – people who garden once a week – and the Royal Horticultural Society has 300,000 members. There are 250,000 allotment holders in the UK. About £6.9 billion is spent on DIY a year and 63 per cent of adults did some kind of DIY in 1999. Some of these are very serious: 20,000 new homes each year are built by self-builders.

While engagement with formal politics has declined, participation in single issue campaigns has risen. In 2000, 53 per cent of people said they took part in some kind of political activity, up from 44 per cent in 1986. This cuts across the political spectrum. In 2002, 400,000 people marched through London against a ban on fox hunting. In 2003, one million people marched against the war in Iraq. Even so, participation in formal politics is still significant. There are perhaps 20,000 local government councillors, for example. Trade Union membership is sustained by perhaps 250,000 largely Pro-Am workplace representatives.

The Demos Pro-Am survey

Our estimate is that perhaps 58 per cent of the British population engage in some kind of activity that could be described as Pro-Am. That is the proportion of the population who engage in an amateur

Table 3. Total Pro-Am activity as a proportion of the population as a whole (%)

Activity	Proportion (%)
doing a Pro-Am activity	58
doing 1–2 Pro-Am activities	49
doing 3–4 Pro-Am activities	8
doing 5+ Pro-Am activities	1

activity regularly and rate their skills as reasonably good: they see themselves as Pro-Ams. This estimate, based on self-assessment of skills, may be an overestimate. The true, 'hard-core' Pro-Am population is likely to be a subset of this. But even if that were a half of the total Pro-Am group identified in our survey, that would still mean at least 25 per cent of the population see themselves as Pro-Am.

Our survey found that 49 per cent of the population engage in one or two Pro-Am activities, 8 per cent engage in three or four and 1 per cent engage in five of more (see Table 3). If we were to use this as a basis for measuring the Pro-Am group it would be between 9 per cent and 49 per cent of the population.

These estimates of the scale of Pro-Am activity come from a MORI survey of 2,189 British adults completed in June 2004. MORI first asked people which – from a list of 20 activities – they did regularly, ranging from gardening and DIY to volunteering and nature conservancy. Those people who reported doing an activity regularly were then asked whether they had a good level of skill at the activity. The first is a measure of overall participation and the second a crude measure of many of those are Pro-Ams.

There are drawbacks to this approach. Men seem more likely to say they are good at something than women. DIY is an activity mainly undertaken by men and 74 per cent of those doing DIY rate their skills as good. Women dominate gardening and only 61 per cent of those doing gardening regularly report their skills as good. So this

Measuring the Pro-Am sector

self-assessment exercise is a first approximation of the scale of Pro-Am activity. A summary is seen in Table 4 below.

Table 4. The extent of participation in selected amateur activities, the proportion of respondents reporting 'good skills' and the proportion of the population as a whole who are Pro-Ams.

Activities	Regularly participate (%)	Report good skills (%)	Pro-Ams in population as a whole (%)
Gardening/allotments	30	61	18
DIY	20	74	15
Member of a sports team	12	80	9
Arts (eg painting or drawing) and crafts (eg pottery, carpentry)	11	73	8
Photography	10	58	6
Playing a music instrument	8	72	6
Voluntary work for a local group (parents association, Neighbourhood Watch)	6	68	4
Voluntary work for an organisation (eg St John Ambulance, Samaritans)	5	74	4
Writing (fiction or non-fiction)	6	66	4
Being a mechanic	4	76	3
Fishing	4	63	3
Helping run a sports team	4	71	3
Local/family history	5	56	3
Nature conservation	4	49	2
Therapies (eg reflexology, aromatherapy)	4	58	2
Training/breeding pets	3	65	2
Amateur dramatics	1	65	1
Choir singing	2	68	1
Maintaining a website	2	61	1
Political campaigning	1	52	1

Table 4. *continued*

Activities	Regularly participate (%)	Report good skills (%)	Pro-Ams in population as a whole (%)
None of these	33	11	42
Don't know	1	1	1
Refused	–	–	–

The most popular Pro-Am activities by far are gardening (30 per cent say they do it regularly, 61 per cent say they have skills of a good standard, which means 18 per cent of the population see themselves as Pro-Am gardeners) and DIY (20 per cent say they do it regularly, 74 per cent say they have good skills, which means 15 per cent of the population see themselves as Pro-Am at do-it-yourself.) About 16 per cent are involved in playing sports as a member of a team or running a sports team, with 12 per cent of the population claiming Pro-Am skills in sports. The arts make up a large category: 11 per cent say they engage in arts and crafts, 10 per cent in photography, 6 per cent in writing, 1 per cent in amateur dramatics and 2 per cent in singing. Overall perhaps 30 per cent of the population claim Pro-Am arts skills of one kind or another. About 11 per cent engage in voluntary work, either locally or for a national organisation like St John Ambulance, and 8 per cent of the population as a whole see themselves as Pro-Am volunteers.

The growth of Pro-Am activity does not necessarily imply stronger social capital. Many of the most popular Pro-Am activities can be quite individualistic: gardening, DIY, writing, photography, playing a musical instrument. Other Pro-Am activities – volunteering, campaigning, organising sports and social clubs – are more social. This basic distinction between 'private' Pro-Ams (gardening, DIY, writing) and 'social' Pro-Ams (volunteering, club organisers, performers) will be important in guiding policies to promote different kinds of Pro-Am activities.

Participation in Pro-Am activities is heavily slanted towards well-educated, middle class people with incomes above £30,000 per year. There are some exceptions to this: fishing, for example, is largely a working class pastime. In some activities – volunteering for example – the class balance is more mixed. But as a rule people with financial, social and educational resources are far more likely to engage in Pro-Am activities than those without these resources, as Table 5 below shows.

Those who engage in activities as a Pro-Ams are likely to be wealthy and better educated (see Tables 6 and 7).

Employment status is a less important factor than income, in part because retired people with incomes in excess of £30,000 a year may be a significant part of the Pro-Am population. Different Pro-Am activities seem to be combined with different working patterns. Elderly people and those not working play a disproportionately large

Table 5. Pro-Ams and social class

Social class	% of total partipants
AB	72
C1	61
C2	58
DE	43
Total Pro-Ams (as per cent of population)	58

Table 6. Pro-Ams and education level

Education level	% of total participants
Degree	70
A levels	69
GCSE	55
No qualifications	43
Total Pro-Ams (as per cent of population)	58

Table 7. Pro-Ams and household income

Household income level	% of total participants
£30,000+	70
£17,500–29,999	60
up to £17,500	49
Total Pro-Ams (as per cent of population)	58

role in gardening, but not in DIY, which is concentrated among working age men in full-time employment. People not working or working part-time are far more likely to be Pro-Am artists than people working full time. In contrast Pro-Am sports people are more likely to be in full-time employment. Part-time workers are more likely to become Pro-Am volunteers than either full-timers or those who are not working (see Table 8).

The other striking feature is the gender divide in Pro-Am activities. Having children in the household is not a major factor in whether people engage in Pro-Am pursuits; 57 per cent of people with children see themselves as Pro-Ams as do 59 per cent of those without children. Engaging in time-consuming, Pro-Am activities, is compatible with having children.

The explanation for this may be found in the gender split for Pro-

Table 8. Pro-Ams and employment

Employment	% of total participants
Full-time	61
Part-time	62
Not working	43
Total Pro-Ams (as per cent of population)	58

Am activities. Men are far more likely to be Pro-Ams than women: 66 per cent of men claim some kind of Pro-Am skill compared with 50 per cent of women. Moreover women are more likely to engage in Pro-Am activities that revolve around the home: gardening, writing and the arts. Men are more likely to engage in activities that take them away from home, sports, for example, as well as doing some home-based activities, such as DIY. In some areas there is a rough gender balance: family history, pets, nature conservancy.

Not only are women less likely to become Pro-Ams, their range of Pro-Am activities is probably more constrained, especially when they have children. They tend to build their Pro-Am careers more around home and family, whereas men are likely to engage in both home-based Pro-Am work and activities that take them away from home quite regularly. Indeed, for some women the intensity of their partner's Pro-Am activities is likely to be an additional strain in their lives.

Age is not a major factor in Pro-Am participation but the activities people get involved in are segregated by age (see Table 9).

The young tend to dominate in music and sports, while older people are more likely to be Pro-Am gardeners and volunteers. Participation in arts and crafts is evenly spread. DIY activities are concentrated among working age men.

Table 9. Pro-Ams and age

Age range	% of total participants
15–24	56
25–34	55
35–44	62
45–54	64
55+	56
Total Pro-Ams (as per cent of population)	58

Table 10. Pro-Am regional rankings

Ranking	Region	% of total participants
1	Eastern	68
2	Yorks/Humb	67
3	South West	66
4	South East	63
5	North West	57
6	West Mids	55
6	Wales	55
7	London	53
8	East Mids	47
9	Scotland	45
Total Pro-Ams		58

There also seem to be marked regional differences in the level of Pro-Am activity. Table 10 shows the overall regional ranking for Pro-Am activity.

For all the limitations of this initial attempt to estimate the size of the Pro-Am sector in society the main conclusions are striking.

o The Pro-Ams are a significant social force: 58 per cent of the population see themselves as Pro-Ams.

o However, participation is heavily weighted towards middle class, well-educated and reasonably affluent people. Once working class people participate in an activity they are as likely as middle class people to become Pro-Am by acquiring the necessary skills. The issue is not acquiring the skills but access and participation in the first place. If more working class people were able to participate more would become Pro-Ams.

o Men are more likely to become Pro-Ams than women, in part because women are more likely to take responsibility for childcare. Women's Pro-Am activities tend to be compatible with being at home or looking after children. Men are far more likely to engage in Pro-Am activities that take them away from the house.

○ All ages participate as Pro-Ams but their activities tend to be age specific: older people garden, while younger people tend to be drawn to sports and arts.

○ Some regions seem to have strong Pro-Am cultures: the East, Yorkshire and South West, while in others, particularly Scotland and the East Midlands, Pro-Am culture is far less developed. London is relatively weak in Pro-Am activities.

We will take up the implications of these findings for public policy in a later chapter.

I used to say I was a counsellor. But now I say I am a garden designer. It was when I had designed my first garden from scratch and seen it built that I realised. I had really done it. It was a wonderful moment, seeing all these ingredients coming together. I had made my mark. After that I knew I was doing it, not just dreaming about it.

Dilip Lakhani, Pro-Am garden designer

I am always looking for something harder, something new to do and when you are climbing it's a very solo activity, it's just you and the face. You get a very focused sense of challenge and achievement.

Brendan Sheehan, Pro-Am mountain climber

I've often thought I'd like to do it full time. But maybe I'm so enthusiastic because it's not my day job. Maybe I'd lose something by going full time. Things you do in your spare time are always more exciting aren't they?

Andrew Greenwood, Pro-Am astronomer

I love problem-solving and if you are into software then pretty much the only way you do that is by getting involved in open source because proprietary systems are closed. For me it's like doing vast jigsaw puzzles. Open source communities are very meritocratic. They judge you on your ideas and contribution. So if you have good ideas you get recognised.

Seb Potter, Pro-Am open source programmer

4. The Pro-Am ethic

People have shadow careers as Pro-Ams, with highs and low, frustrations and achievements. A Pro-Am systematically pursues an amateur activity that is substantial enough for the participant to acquire knowledge and skills over a long period. A Pro-Am career is not to be undertaken lightly.

Being a hard-core Pro-Am takes dedication, passion and perseverance. Pro-Ams report their activities involve anxiety, risk, struggle and setbacks, as well as substantial investments of time and money.

The skills required develop only over time, and their acquisition usually needs to be systematic: it involves learning from coaches and peers. The knowledge involved is invariably substantial, in the sense that it involves several layers of technique. It cannot be picked up quickly or casually, and requires social organisation through which skills can be shared, passed on and accredited, through clubs, networks, events, competitions and performances. Pro-Ams put their time and money in many different things – equipment, props, technology, travelling to and from events, club memberships. What all this amounts to is a substantial investment in 'cultural capital'.

The term 'cultural capital' was coined by the French sociologist Pierre Bourdieu in his 1985 book *Distinction: a social critique of the judgement of taste*.[19] Bourdieu argued that people have four different kinds of 'capital' at their disposal: financial, human (knowledge and skills), social (connections and relationships) and cultural. By cultural capital he meant: the ability to take part in cultural activities, not just highbrow culture but everything from sports and hobbies, attending evening courses or visiting an exhibition, going to a museum or seeing a play. These activities signal what is important to you and so what kind of person you are. Bourdieu argued that people assemble these four kinds of capital in different ways to create a distinctive lifestyle and identity. Cultural capital is what makes us stand out as individuals. Pro-Ams are rich in cultural capital.

As Jonathan Gershuny, Professor of Sociology at University of Essex puts it: 'Specific knowledge about consumption contributes to individual satisfaction with consumption. Having the knowledge necessary to participate in an activity is closely correlated with the desire to do so.'[20] To enjoy going to see a film, one might only need the time and the money to visit a cinema. To join a film club requires more than time and money: it depends on a strong desire to learn more about film and to identify yourself with a community of fellow film buffs. The more we learn, the more confident we become about an activity – astronomy, playing tennis, acting – and so the more pleasure we are likely to get from it. Consumption becomes a knowledge-intensive activity.

Pro-Ams enjoy acquiring cultural capital: they enjoy immersion in a body of knowledge held by a community. But it's not just one way. They also like passing it on, being part of a flow of knowledge through a community. Many of the Pro-Ams teach others, or informally pass on skills to peers. As Jeremy Rifkin put it in *The Age of Access*: 'In an era where cultural production is becoming the dominant form of economic activity, securing access to the many cultural resources and experiences which nurture one's psychological existence becomes just as important as holding onto property.'[21]

As the investment is significant, so the benefits to the individual have to be durable: a lasting sense of identity, achievement and satisfaction. Pro-Ams get far more intense, pleasurable and satisfying experiences from their activities than they do from work, formal learning or passive consumption. Pro-Ams feel more themselves and more fulfilled when they engage in these activities.

Psychologist Graham Privette, in his study of the satisfaction from leisure found that people who have more 'serious' pursuits are more likely to feel focus, a sense of power, joy, value, integration and wholeness than those who consume by shopping. The people in Privette's study reported having 'peak' experiences from 'peak' performances while engaged in serious leisure.[22] Pro-Ams report just these deeply concentrated experiences.

Participation in serious leisure improves health and well-being. Pro-Am leisure activities generate more social benefits pound-for-pound than passive and casual leisure. This is born out by a study of more than 5,000 Scottish teenagers, which found that where opportunities for challenging and rewarding leisure were limited, their psychological health suffered. Young women were significantly more at risk than young men of falling prey to depression and low self-esteem if they did not have serious leisure pursuits. Young people who see serious leisure as central to their lives are more likely to have a high sense of self-esteem.

Another study by psychologist Michael Argyle found that the more that people described their leisure activities as stressful and challenging, the more likely they were to be absorbed and satisfied by them.[23] A recent report by the UK Government's Strategy Unit, for example, found that people who exercise regularly are markedly more satisfied with their lives than those that rarely exercise.[24] The difference is even more marked for people who regularly work in their gardens and those who regularly attend meetings of local groups. Pro-Ams allow serious play a significant role in their lives: they are not workaholics.[25]

Pro-Am activities also bring social benefits for those involved. They have a sense of self-worth and a place in society. Vertical social mobility – measured by income and wealth – has not become markedly easier in modern Britain. Yet horizontal social mobility – the opportunity for people to adopt different lifestyles according to their interests – has increased a great deal, at all levels of income, as society has become better off. Limited vertical social mobility, combined with massive horizontal social mobility, creates a society that is simultaneously more fluid and open than it was, while being just as stratified. Pro-Ams are horizontally mobile through their acquisition and deployment of cultural capital.[26]

That cultural capital also provides them with a sense of belonging. Pro-Ams need other members of their community to learn from, play with, compete against, perform to. Pro-Am organisations help to generate social capital, lasting relationships and friendships, that help to provide a social glue and basis for cooperation. Pro-Am tribes could become more important as the traditional family and local communities decline. As local community has dwindled as a source of common identity, so knowledge has become more important. Six out of ten people say they have more in common with people they share a hobby with than their neighbours, according to the Henley Centre study done for the Discovery Channel.[27] Local communities thrived not just on proximity but shared viewpoints. These days we engage with people who share our view of the world without having to live next door to them. Sharing Pro-Am knowledge and interests is the new basis for community.

People with Pro-Am skills tend to be more resilient. A shadow Pro-Am career is a form of insurance: everyone should have Pro-Am skills to fall back on should their formal and professional career run into the sand and leave them stranded. When Audrey Miller's teaching career ran into the sand with budget cuts, she turned to her Pro-Am skills to create a second career as a campaigner. Dilip Lakhani got his first job in the NHS through skills he acquired as a volunteer on the AIDS Helpline. Having reached the top of his NHS career ladder, his emerging second career revolves around his interest in gardening.

When you are in the run up to an event you are working really intensively, the whole time. We are just organising for World Debt Day now and I am working seven days a week on it. But one of the benefits of being an amateur is that you can stop when you want to, which you could not do if it was a job or you were in an office. When it all gets too much I can take myself off to the allotment. It's much more flexible like that.

Audrey Miller, Pro-Am campaigner

In the old days there was a structure to the industry that you could follow. As a young actor you would go into rep theatre in the regions and then work your way up to London and the West End. But as rep theatre has contracted its role has been replaced by the London fringe. But on the fringe you often only get paid through a profit share. Which means if there is no profit you get no money. Which means that many people who call themselves professional actors are actually doing it for the love of it and not because they are being paid.

Alison Maguire, Pro-Am actor

It was very simple. We just exchanged emails and agreed it was a good thing to do. We divided up the tasks among us depending on who could do what and within a month we had a fully functioning website which people could visit to get tips and advice to make life easier if you were developing a website. We just wanted to make it easier to solve problems.

Seb Potter, Pro-Am open source programmer

5. How Pro-Ams organise

Hard-core Pro-Am activities are often social in nature: Pro-Ams do it with one another, often in public. It is virtually impossible to engage in a Pro-Am activity solo.

Five aspects of Pro-Am activities require social organisation:

- learning and the transmission of skills, through classes and courses, rehearsals and training sessions
- accreditation through exams, grading competitions and auditions
- peer recognition through events, displays and performances
- social bonding through social activities that underscore common codes of dress, behaviour and values
- representation of members' views to the wider community and society at large.

Pro-Am organisations vary considerably. Local branches and clubs may have become less important in organising these activities than they once were. This may well reflect the decline of commitment to a highly organised sense of local community. However the careers of our Pro-Ams suggests that clubs may be in decline in part because other kinds of organisation may better fulfil some of the functions once undertaken by clubs. Forty years ago clubs performed all five of the roles set out above. Nowadays, Pro-Ams use networks, alongside the traditional club, to coordinate their activities. They are creatures of digital technologies, niche media and specialist branding. They use their mobile telephones and the internet to organise physical, face-to-face activities. The organisational burden that once might have been borne by a club, with its office holders, is now often borne by networked digital technologies. Modern Pro-Ams are direct beneficiaries of these 'group forming network technologies'.[28]

These organisational forms and tools are listed below.

The internet: Pro-Ams are avid consumers of specialist websites that feed their hobbies, providing information, advice, knowledge and contacts. They often use the internet to buy equipment and book events.

Messaging: Pro-Ams thrive on messaging systems that allow people to remain in contact even when they are not able to be together. Alison Maguire, for example, organises the Tower Theatre, in part by using email while at work, allowing her to remain in touch and pick up messages.

Media: Pro-Ams are beneficiaries of the explosion of specialist magazines, catering to specialist tastes and interests. Twenty years ago WH Smith was the main source of a limited range of magazines, catering to a limited number of hobbies. Now Borders carries in excess of 900 magazine titles. The number of magazine titles published in the UK rose from 2,042 in 1988 to close to 2,500 by the end of the 1990s. The number of television channels rose from four to more than 60; commercial radio stations went from 60 to 188 and CD-ROM titles from 390 to 16,762.

Brands: Many Pro-Am activities have become brand zones. People display their attachment to climbing or cycling, surfing or skiing by wearing particular brands of clothing. Consumer technology groups, such as camera companies, now market Pro-Am products that meet professional standards. These products may appeal to people who have just taken up an activity and want to display their commitment. Many of the mature Pro-Ams we interviewed were 'brand sceptics'. Their deep knowledge of their activity meant they assessed products on their performance rather than brand. This may have implications for brands that depend on word of mouth marketing. Pro-Ams are often practitioners and teachers: their word could influence others in their community.

Alliances with professionals: In some Pro-Am fields professionals play an important role in helping to mobilise a Pro-Am community. A good example, which might have a bearing on other areas of public policy, is the Territorial Army (see Box 1).

Box 1. The Pro-Am Army

For most of modern history the British army was a Pro-Am organisation. It was only in the nineteenth and twentieth centuries that it became professional. Before that, lords, lairds, nobles and monarchs raised armies from among the local community. Even when the regular army became professionalised the amateur tradition remained important, for instance in the role of the Home Guard during the Second World War and more recently the Territorial Army (TA).[29]

Some historians trace the roots of the auxiliary, volunteer and militia to Anglo-Saxon traditions of communal military obligation that became transformed into medieval law and then into the statutes that set up the people's militia in 1558. The obligation to serve in the militia was imposed upon owners of property in 1757 and it then became a tax on employer manpower in 1831. By the early twentieth century the militia, imperial yeomanry and auxiliary forces were merged to form the territorial forces, the precursor to today's TA.

From the sixteenth century onwards a large standing army was

---

discouraged, as a military despotism was feared. In the Second World War illustrious members of the Home Guard, among them JB Priestley and George Orwell, stressed the democratic and egalitarian nature of the auxiliary forces that embraced a far wider cross-section of society than the regular army.

In *The Amateur Military Tradition*, Ian Beckett describes the definitive history of the auxiliaries: 'Auxiliary forces have been the real point of contact between army and society in Britain. Auxiliaries provided opportunity. This might be the opportunity of experiencing something different or of enjoying recreational facilities or comradeship, which might not otherwise have been enjoyed.'[30] It was also, he noted, a route for social advancement and acceptance into society.

Much of this is still echoed in the way the TA presents itself: as an organisation that provides challenge and comradeship, as well as the opportunity to learn skills that will stand people in good stead in their working lives. At their peak in the late nineteenth century the auxiliary forces accounted for perhaps 6 per cent of the male population aged between 15 and 35. Close to two million men passed through the voluntary forces and militia during the last decades of the nineteenth century. The TA has just 40,000 members. For most of its members, the TA is a parallel career. Every TA member has 8–10 weeks' training, with officers going on a two-week programme at Sandhurst. Most members devote at least 28 days a year to the TA and for that they get a £1,500 'bounty'. Most TA members give up weekends and holidays for training in excess of the standard 28 days. Local TA branches are supported by members of the regular, professional army.

The Territorial Army is a hybrid, Pro-Am organisation: a local, largely volunteer force, supported by professional soldiers and tightly linked with the professional army. The TA provides one model for how the state and professionals can foster Pro-Am forms of organisation that create public value.

Organisation has become a lot easier with email. We have to organise ourselves while also doing our day jobs but cannot be on the phone the whole time talking about theatre. Email allows us to combine our work with organising these activities outside work. It has helped us enormously.

Alison Maguire, Pro-Am actor

A couple of years ago I had some serious health problems but I could carry on organising working from home because these days there is a great deal you can do with a phone and a computer. Email is particularly powerful for connecting and organising people. Let me give you an example. We were preparing some worship material for World Debt Day and a friend of mine in Birmingham translated it into Portuguese. She sent it to friends of hers in Portugal by email and by the end of the day people in Brazil were downloading it from a website there. From Birmingham to Brazil in the space of a single day.

Audrey Miller, Pro-Am campaigner

The internet has become absolutely vital to the whole enterprise of astronomy and is a key tool for allowing amateurs to collaborate with professionals. You often get pros asking amateurs to keep an eye on particular events so they can be sure that everything gets spotted.

Andrew Greenwood, Pro-Am astronomer

6. How society benefits from Pro-Ams

With more Pro-Ams in a society there will be more innovation, deeper social capital and healthier democracy.

Social benefits

Social Pro-Ams help to build social capital: networks of relationships that allow people to collaborate, share ideas and take risks together. Social capital can help glue a society together and allow people to trust one another more easily, thus helping them to adjust to change collaboratively and share risks. Bonding social capital brings people together in the same community or income bracket and so excludes other people. Bridging social capital helps to bring together people from different backgrounds. As Robert Putnam, puts it in *Bowling Alone*:[31] 'Bonding social capital constitutes a kind of sociological superglue, whereas bridging social capital provides a sociological WD-40.' Bonding social capital creates strong in-group loyalties that may also create antagonism among those seemingly excluded. Bridging social capital links people from different backgrounds and provides social lubrication.

Pro-Ams can create both kinds of social capital. They create strong bonds around their interests, but because these interests span different communities they can link people from very different walks of life. As Pro-Am actor Alison Maguire says:

If you are with professional actors there are only three subjects of conversation. First, why your agent is no good. Second, what you are in next. Third, who else you know in the industry. Well, as an aspirant actor new to the professional game I did not have much to say on those subjects, so conversation became rather stilted. Professional actors may be great on stage but fundamentally they are dull. Amateur actors on the other hand have a life and they have something to say about the world outside the theatre.

Pro-Am campaigner Audrey Miller sees great benefits in the diversity of people she has met through what she does:

I've met far more people that I would have done on my allotment. This is not a social network: we don't socialise a lot. But I've met an entire network of campaigners from other campaigning organisations. I have also met lots of young people who I would not have met before. And I've found the contacts with other faiths very inspiring, the Sikh and Muslim communities. Exploring the values we share has been very exciting and one of the most worthwhile things we've done. That gives you a fundamental sense of social connection.

These social benefits may be particularly important for people over the age of 45. Our interviews with Pro-Ams highlighted how many came back to a 'parallel' or 'shadow' career later in life, as their first, formal and professional career came to an end. Audrey Miller, a professional teacher, became a Pro-Am political activist in her 50s, something she had been doing as a volunteer all her life. Dilip Lakhani had wanted to work in gardens all his life but only took up a Pro-Am career as a garden designer once he had reached the top of his formal career ladder. Alison Maguire is planning her retirement around her Pro-Am theatre activities. As society ages and the healthy lifespan expands, so it will become more important for people to be able to engage in stretching and challenging Pro-Am activities in later life.

Economics

Pro-Ams play an increasingly critical economic role, particularly as a source of innovation. As Howard Rheingold puts it in *Smart Mobs*: 'As with the personal computer and the internet, key breakthroughs won't come from established industry leaders but from the fringes, from skunkworks and startups and even associations of amateurs. *Especially* associations of amateurs.'[32]

Amateurs have a long track record of innovation, especially in emerging fields which are too young for there to be an organised and professional body of knowledge or too marginal to warrant the attention of companies or universities.

Jenny Uglow's *The Lunar Men*,[33] a history of the inventions that paved the way for the Industrial Revolution in the eighteenth and nineteenth centuries, is a story of a group of Pro-Am inventors, scientists and manufacturers – Mathew Boulton, Josiah Wedgewood, Erasmus Darwin, James Watt, Joseph Priestley and others. Most were non-conformists and freethinkers, who pursued scientific questions out of curiosity. That tradition of Pro-Am experimentation is alive and well today among open source and hacker communities on the internet or the Homebrew Computer Club, which spawned Steve Jobs's and Steve Wozniak's ideas for a personal computer. Another example of how Pro-Ams lead innovation to create entirely new industries is windsurfing.[34]

In Hawaii in the 1970s, top amateur windsurfers were trying to outdo one another by jumping from the top of large waves. Invariably, they fell off in mid-air because they could not keep their feet on the board. Then two of the leading protagonists, Larry Stanley and Mike Horgan, decided to try a different approach. Several years before, Stanley had built an experimental board with footstraps. Next he adapted it for jumping. 'I could go so much faster than I ever thought,' Stanley recalled. 'When you hit a wave it was like a motorcycle rider hitting a ramp; you just flew into the air . . . and you could land the thing and change direction. Within a couple of days ten other people had boards with improvised straps.'[35]

The idea was fast-spreading. High performance windsurfing started from that 'amateur' innovation. By 1998 more than a million people were taking part in the sport that Stanley and Horgan created.

Pro-Ams play three distinct roles in innovation.

First, Pro-Ams can be disruptive innovators. Disruptive innovation changes the way an industry operates by creating new ways of doing business, often by making products and services much cheaper or by creating entirely new products. Disruptive innovation often starts in marginal, experimental markets rather than mainstream mass markets. Embryonic markets are often too small to sustain traditional approaches to R & D. That is where Pro-Ams come in. Dedicated amateurs pursue new ideas even when it appears there is no money to be made. That is why they are a persistent source for disruptive innovations, such as Rap music.

Second, Pro-Ams lead innovation in use. The more technologically radical the innovation the more difficult it is to say in advance what the innovation is for. It may be impossible for the 'authors' of the innovation to predict exactly how it will be used. It is down to the consumers to work out what a new technology is really *for*. That requires innovation in use or the co-creation of value between consumers and producers. Mastering a computer game used to be an individualistic activity undertaken by boys in the dark of their bedrooms. Now it's a mass team sport that depends on intense collaboration. By 2000, most strategy-based computer games had built-in tools to allow players to create and customise the content and action. Knowledge about the game is constantly developing among a sprawling army of Pro-Am players, linked by websites and chat rooms. A game's official release is the moment when the initiative passes from the in-house developers to the community of Pro-Am users. There is a sound commercial logic behind this encouragement of Pro-Am innovation. Open, mass innovation allows many innovations to continue in parallel once a game has been released among a distributed community. If a game sells one million copies and just one per cent of the players are Pro-Am developers, that creates an R & D team of 10,000 people working on further developments. Their contributions make the game more interesting and that in turn extends the game's life, constantly refreshing it.

Third, Pro-Ams are vital to service innovation. All services are delivered to a script, which directs the parts played by the actors involved. Most service innovation comes from producers and users simultaneously adopting a new script, playing out new and complementary roles in the story. That explains why the 'script' for ordering a meal in a formal restaurant – replete with waiters, tips, menus – is so different from the 'script' for ordering in a self-service restaurant, when the consumer does much of the basic labour involved. Pro-Am consumers play a critically important role in devising these new scripts, because they are the leading, more informed and assertive consumers.[36]

Harnessing Pro-Am service innovators will be vital to the future of public services, especially in health, social care and education. As an example take diabetes. Surveys show that most people prefer to have health issues dealt with at home rather than having to visit a hospital or surgery. Surveys of diabetes sufferers also show that those who are more able to self-manage their condition are less likely to suffer health crises than those with little know-how who rely on specialist help. One of the most effective ways to improve the lives of diabetes sufferers is to equip them better to self-manage their condition, to write their own scripts on how they want their condition treated.

The more Pro-Am skills there are distributed across an economy the greater the innovation and labour market flexibility.

Democratic benefits

The more Pro-Ams there are in a society the healthier its democracy is likely to be. While participation in formal politics and membership of political parties has declined, there has been a parallel massive growth in single issue and pressure group campaigns. These networked campaigns – from the Jubilee Debt Campaign, to the anti-globalisation movement, Friends of the Earth and the Countryside Alliance – are often organised by largely Pro-Am organisations. These campaigns often have a huge media impact that belies their fragile organisations. Analysis of network-based campaigning shows these Pro-Am organisations have light structures and small central secretariats, they build coalitions around simple common goals and deploy digital technology to network people together.[37] The Jubilee 2000 website, for example, could send emails to more than 12,000 people, who in turn passed information to many others. In four years, Jubilee 2000 grew from being a UK-based organisation with a single employee working from a shed near London's South Bank to being an international force, with 69 national campaigns and 24 million signatures to a petition which led to the cancellation of US$36 billion of debt. Ultimately these bottom-up, Pro-Am forms of organisation are cheaper, more agile and more fun than formally structured parties.

The fact that people can pursue amateur hobbies and interests without state censorship or interference is a good measure of freedom. People with passions that draw them into civic life are more likely to have a stake in a democratic process that defends this freedom of association. As Freeman Dyson the physicist put it in a *New York Review of Books* article: 'In almost all the varied walks of life, amateurs have more freedom to experiment and innovate. The fraction of a population who are amateurs is a good measure of the freedom of a society.'[38]

I love my job. I've been doing it now for 11 years and I am not bored and I am not frustrated. But the 40s are looming and a couple of years ago I started thinking quite consciously about what my next step would be, what would I move up to from counselling. I had reached the top of the career ladder in counselling. I could become a psychoanalyst or psychotherapist, but that would require a lot more training. I could become a more senior manager but that does not appeal. Or I could stick with my current job and start doing something different alongside it, something I have always wanted to do: design gardens. So although I am not bored now, I am not learning as much as I used to on the job and I don't want to get stale. The solution is to carry on doing the mainstream job, but to build up my gardening on the side. I still do a very professional job at work but my passion is really in the gardening.

Dilip Lakhani, Pro-Am garden designer

7. Pro-Am policy issues

A society with a higher proportion of Pro-Ams should have better mental and physical health, stronger social capital, more innovation and labour market flexibility and a livelier democracy. Should public policy be redirected to promote these spillovers?

The emergence and growth of Pro-Am culture has less to do with public policy than a set of underlying social and demographic factors:

- the expanding life span (people are living between 10 and 20 years longer than they did 40 years ago)
- growing levels of education
- a more open society in which people want a sense of individual fulfilment
- the spread of horizontal social mobility as people develop distinctive lifestyles
- changes in occupational patterns which mean that people are increasingly likely to turn to second careers in their 40s and 50s
- increasing affluence, and an apparent willingness to downshift, trading income for time and better quality of life.

All of these are creating a more complex and varied life-cycle, which in turn creates new opportunities for Pro-Am activity.

The main goal of public policy should be relatively modest: to avoid policy interventions that might stifle the growth in Pro-Am activity. Powerful social and economic trends are likely to promote Pro-Am culture, without government intervention.

Many of the factors that encourage Pro-Am activity – income and education – will be more widely spread within the next 15 years. By 2020, mean household income is projected to be more than £44,000, up from about £27,000 in 2002. Leisure spending is rising as a proportion of total consumer spending. In 1999, consumer spending on leisure and services surpassed spending on material goods for the first time, having been only half as much 30 years ago. Spending on serious and active leisure is part of this general leisure spend. Future generations are likely to be better educated. More than 50 per cent of men over the age of 65 have no educational qualifications, compared with less than 10 per cent of those under the age of 30.[39]

The extended lifespan should give people longer, healthier lives allowing them more time for second and third careers, after their children have grown up. A woman born in 1850 would have had little time for herself. A woman born in 1950, whose eldest child reached 18 in the 1980s, might have 30 years of healthy life without direct child care responsibilities. By 2020 there will be five million more people in the UK population over the age of 45, a prime group for many Pro-Am activities.

Pro-Am activity thrives in an open, liberal, well-educated, affluent and democratic society, in which people have enough time outside work and the resources they need to cultivate their Pro-Am activities. Public policy interventions such as the expansion of higher education will matter but only in the context of these larger social trends.

However, public policy could play a critical role in making Pro-Am activities more accessible to those who currently have few opportunities to participate. A large share of Pro-Am activities – gardening, DIY, some arts activities – are not social but private. One aim of government policy might be to encourage greater socialisation around some of these activities. There are significant inequalities in people's ability to engage in Pro-Am activities. Well-educated men, with incomes in excess of £30,000 a year, are far more likely to engage in these activities than women with few qualifications on low incomes. People who cannot participate in Pro-Am activities are excluded from the benefits that serious leisure brings. Inequalities in income are compounded by inequalities in the kinds of leisure experiences people can engage in. Beyond these distributional questions, the increasingly important role Pro-Ams play in labour market flexibility and innovation should be reflected in economic policy.

Socialising Pro-Am culture

Despite the rhetoric of 'building social capital', the government knows remarkably little about which policies help to generate social ties.[40] In a complex society, the best government can hope for is *not* to introduce policies that destroy social capital. Yet investment in Pro-Ams could make policies designed to promote social capital far more effective by grounding them in the lived experience of ordinary people. Few people set out to build social capital. Most people join a club to pursue an activity they enjoy – to rock climb, act or play with computers. Social capital is an unintended by-product of these activities. Pro-Am enthusiasts organise the networks and clubs that breathe life into otherwise empty community halls. Community centres are social capital hardware; Pro-Ams provide the software.

The government's community programmes, the New Deal for Communities for example, should invest in Pro-Ams as well as infrastructure. The government should launch a Pro-Am fellowship programme, investing small sums in community Pro-Ams. This might be modelled on localised versions of the National Endowment for Science Technology and the Arts, which provide fellowships for innovators, and be funded by the Big Lottery Fund.

Encouraging social rather than private Pro-Am activities could be an important part of the response to changing demographics. More people will be living on their own in future through choice as well as force of circumstance. By 2021, the largest household groups will be couples with no children and people under pensionable age living on their own. Their growth could help fuel Pro-Am culture, if, as Manuel Castells predicts, this demand for isolation is accompanied by a need to find new common identities.[41]

Pro-Ams could help to revolutionise public services. A wider range of public institutions – from public libraries to the BBC, schools and hospitals – will become more effective by growing a Pro-Am constituency around them, a kind of guerrilla army of advisers, helpers and innovators to amplify the impact of a professional service. Since the creation of the welfare state, public services have been defined by the professionals who deliver them: more education means more teachers; better healthcare means more doctors and nurses; lower crime means more police. Given the costs of employing professionals and the low productivity of many public services, it has often been very difficult to expand service provision without incurring higher wage costs.

To get around this bottleneck, public service 'professionals' should increasingly work alongside para-professionals and assistants – in classrooms, on the beat, in social care and hospital wards. Voluntary bodies that recruit, motivate and train these para-professionals will become increasingly important. Age Concern, which provides thousands of social care volunteers, is a prime example. Negotiating with professionals to loosen their grip on knowledge, accreditation and job descriptions will be vital to long-term reform to public services.

Bodies such as the NHS increasingly will have to equip users with tools and education to do-it-themselves as well as providing safe spaces and environments in which they can network and learn. An example of what this might involve is the Department of Health's expert-patient programme, which aims to train thousands of sufferers of chronic conditions to become more adept at self-management. A small professional workforce of GPs and nurses should support a vast army of Pro-Am expert-patients advising one another on the non-biomedical aspects of their conditions.

Organisations that have been given responsibility for promoting learning and training within public services, such as the NHS

University, the Teacher Training Agency and Centrex, the police training organisation should look at how they can help develop the capacity of Pro-Ams of various kinds to support the work of professionals. Public libraries, in their twenty-first century incarnation, could play a crucial role as centres for Pro-Am activity. The public sector should tap into Pro-Am values. Public service institutions should be far more able to excite and harness Pro-Am contributions than the private sector. That could be a vital source of future competitive advantage for public sector organisations.

Promoting Pro-Am culture should be a central focus for public service media. A prime example is the BBC's Neighbourhood Gardener scheme, developed with the Royal Horticultural Society, which is modelled on the US Master Gardener scheme, in which 60,000 college-accredited amateur gardeners provide millions of hours of expertise free of charge to other gardeners in their locality. The BBC project, launched in May 2004, aims to provide thousands of dedicated amateur gardeners with nine months' part-time training to develop their teaching and organisational skills so they can 'pass on their horticultural wisdom and enthusiasm to others in their local community'.[42] Public service media should provide people with tools and help to foster networks to encourage them to undertake activities on their own behalf, with other people, from gardening to local history, nature conservation to amateur dramatics.

Addressing Pro-Am inequalities

Affluent people are more likely to participate in Pro-Am activities than those on low incomes. Incomes may in part reflect differences in educational qualifications: someone with a degree or three A levels is far more likely to be a Pro-Am than someone with no qualifications. Men are more likely to be Pro-Am than women, especially women with children. When women do participate they tend to engage in home-based activities that can be scheduled flexibly to fit in with childcare. Men are far more likely to engage in Pro-Am activities that involve a commitment to clubs and activities that take them away from home. Our study confirms the findings of other similar studies that men are far more likely to belong to a voluntary association, hobby group, sports, social or consumer club.[43] To the extent that these 'social' Pro-Am activities bring additional benefits – access to networks, social contacts and support – women are doubly disadvantaged. The group most likely to engage in and organise Pro-Am activities comprises well-educated, relatively affluent men. The group least likely to be Pro-Ams comprises low-income women, with children and few educational qualifications.

These disparities matter because participation in Pro-Am activities, and social Pro-Am activities in particular, bring important benefits, over and above individual satisfaction. They can build community spirit, capacity for cooperation, spread skills and promote trust, as well as provide participants with a sense of self-worth and fulfilment. Groups less able to participate in these activities will be disadvantaged as a result. However, before rushing to design policies to promote more equal access to Pro-Am pastimes, it would be sensible to better understand where these inequalities come from.

Some groups may not participate in Pro-Am activities because

O   they lack a sense of interest and motivation as they do not
      see themselves as the kind of person who undertakes the
      activity in question
O   they have the interest and appetite for an activity but lack
      the financial or educational resources to fulfil them
O   no one asks them to join in because they are not part of
      the relevant social networks
O   even when asked to join in they feel the rules and codes of
      membership, such as when and where the activity takes
      place, do not suit them.

More research is needed to understand the specific combination of factors that deter women, people on low incomes, and those with few qualifications from participating in Pro-Am activities. Clearly, policies designed to promote 'clubs' and traditional social organisations may just reach those already well able to take part in

Pro-Am activities. Novel policies may be required to boost participation by those unlikely to join traditional clubs.

Rising incomes and educational entitlements may gradually erode the social class inequalities in leisure. The single most effective policy intervention may be the expansion of participation in higher education. Policies to promote social Pro-Am activities, such as the BBC Neighbourhood Gardener scheme and Pro-Am advocates in communities, could be tailored for poorer communities. Early investment also pays big dividends. Children who are exposed to cultural experiences – visiting museums, galleries, the theatre – are more likely to build up their cultural capital in later life. Youngsters who take part in volunteering programmes at school are far more likely to continue volunteering later in life. One study found that children exposed to cultural activities and volunteering when young were significantly more likely to develop high levels of human capital and earn more later in life.[44] This suggests it would pay dividends to expand programmes such as Creative Partnerships, which exposes young children to creative learning, making volunteering as much part of mainstream education as science or history. Schools should play an active role in encouraging their students' Pro-Am activities. The Department for Education and Skills (DfES), Department for Culture, Media and Sport (DCMS) and Department of Trade and Industry (DTI) should jointly organise a national programme aimed at 16–21-year-olds who want to spend a year pursuing social Pro-Am activities.

Gender inequalities in Pro-Am activities will be eroded, as they have been in other spheres, by changes in traditional roles played by men and women at home, the expansion of educational opportunities for women and the increase in the proportion of women in managerial and professional jobs. Later marriage, lower fertility and longer lifespans should make Pro-Am careers more of a possibility for women. The provision of a better community childcare network, for example linked to Sure Start schemes, will also help more women to take up Pro-Am activities.

Yet even with these trends it is likely that women will lag behind men in Pro-Am activities. Women now participate as much as men in formal, electoral politics, for example, but men still dominate campaigns and organisations that require major commitments of time.[45] Part of the problem for some women with children is that their Pro-Am opportunities are curtailed because they live with men who choose to pursue demanding Pro-Am careers. It is easier for men to engage in serious leisure than women, especially women who combine work with bringing up children. Rebecca Abrams, in *The Playful Self* argues that women find it harder than men to license themselves to play.[46] This is amply demonstrated in the life stories of Alison Maguire and Audrey Miller, who both compromised their Pro-Am careers for the sake of their family.

Policies to promote female Pro-Ams could include the following ideas.

O   Creating more informal home-based networks of women
     based on book groups or informal parenting support.
     Rather than encourage women to join clubs it would
     make more sense to help build organisations based on
     their informal social networks.
O   Building on the role of Pro-Am organisations such as the
     Women's Royal Voluntary Service (WRVS), the Women's
     Institute and church groups to play wider roles in learning
     and skills development.
O   Building on activities in which women are already well
     represented, such as gardening and local volunteering.
O   Promoting role models of women Pro-Ams, from
     Florence Nightingale to Tracey Morris, the marathon
     runner (and contact lens fitter) who qualified for the
     Olympics based on her performance in the 2004 London
     Marathon.

Time will also be a crucial factor. Working women with children already face enormous time pressures. As working hours lengthen and become more flexible it becomes more difficult for people in employment to engage in regular, planned, social activities. It is difficult to pursue a Pro-Am activity in isolation: you have to find someone to do it *with*.[47] As Jenkins and Osberg put it in their study of working hours and leisure: 'Time spent in isolation is, for most people, only pleasurable in small doses. Many of the things that people do in their non-work time, involve other people, and are distinctly more pleasurable if done with others. However the huge variety of leisure tastes that people have mean that individuals face a problem of locating "somebody to play with" and of scheduling simultaneous free time.' Just as schools have 'games afternoons' so might companies, at least once a month, for serious Pro-Am activities and volunteering. Just as schools and universities hold careers fairs, so might companies organise Pro-Am fairs, in which employees try to engage one another in their favourite pastimes. One bank holiday a year could be designated as a national volunteering day, an opportunity for everyone to showcase their talents and recruit others to their cause. A new project for the open source software movement would be to create a version of the Friendster social networking website as a way of helping people to link up with others with similar interests in their neighbourhoods.[48]

Pro-Ams and economics

Pro-Ams play an increasingly important role in business innovation. This challenges the traditional assumptions of public policy that innovation starts in R & D labs, where backroom boys and boffins come up with bright ideas that they pass down a pipeline to waiting consumers. Traditional innovation policies subsidise R & D and accelerate the transmission of ideas down the pipeline and into the market. Pro-Ams are helping to turn this closed model on its head. In mobile phones, media, computer games and software, ideas are flowing back up the pipeline from avid users to the technology producers. Pro-Ams should play a much larger role in innovation policy. Lead users should play a larger role in foresight exercises to chart the future course of innovation, and policies to deregulate markets should also open up spaces for Pro-Am innovations. Pro-Am communities are the new R & D labs of the digital economy.

The UK is not a large market in global terms, but it could be one of the most creative if policy enables Pro-Am innovation. One specific proposal flows out of the likely freeing up of the radio spectrum over the coming decades, as underused publicly-owned bandwidth is auctioned off and new technologies permit greater sharing and cross-use of different frequencies. Rather than simply letting market forces rip, some spectra should be reserved as an innovation commons for techie Pro-Ams – the kind that helped create the WiFi revolution – to play and experiment with.

No government has yet designed a policy to support open source models of technology development. Most major Pro-Am and open source developments – such as Linux and Apache software – have come from informal groups of Pro-Ams banding together, often based around a university, such as Berkeley near San Francisco. Open source initiatives such as Linux provide a vital alternative to an incumbent proprietary supplier such as Microsoft. An innovation policy to deliberately fund open source communities as competitors to incumbents would look quite different from one modelled on the Silicon Valley venture capital approach to exploiting intellectual capital.

Pro-Am policies should also ease labour mobility. Helping people to prepare for life beyond employment by encouraging them to take up voluntary and Pro-Am activities in their 40s could become a key policy to help sustain people through a long period after the end of their first formal career. Employers should be encouraged to provide people nearing a career change with time off work for Pro-Am development. Helping people develop their shadow Pro-Am career should make it easier for people to cope with the loss of a job. Creating programmes that help people turn their hobbies into small businesses would also help, perhaps by offering in-kind support or preferential treatment – a similar approach has been pioneered very successfully by Brazilian entrepreneur, Ricardo Semler's SemCo. Adults often pick up basic literacy, numeracy and social skills through participation in hobbies and craft activities which provide an entry point into formal education.

In sum our main policy proposals for promoting Pro-Am participation include the ideas listed below.

○ The government's community programmes: the New Deal for Communities for example, should invest in Pro-Ams as well as in infrastructure.

○ The government should launch a Pro-Am fellowship programme, investing small sums in community Pro-Ams. This might be modelled on localised versions of the National Endowment for Science Technology and the Arts, which provide fellowships for innovators, and be funded by the Big Lottery Fund.

○ Public institutions – from public libraries to the BBC, schools and hospitals – will become more effective by growing a Pro-Am constituency around them, a kind of guerrilla army of advisers, helpers and innovators to amplify the impact of a professional service.

○ Organisations that have been given responsibility for promoting learning and training within public services, such as the NHS University, the Teacher Training Agency and Centrex, the police training organisation, should look at how they can help develop the capacity of Pro-Ams of various kinds to support the work of professionals.

○ Promoting Pro-Am culture should be a central focus for public service media. A prime example is the BBC's Neighbourhood Gardener scheme, developed with the Royal Horticultural Society, which is modelled on the US Master Gardener scheme, in which 60,000 college-accredited amateur gardeners provide millions of hours of expertise free of charge to other gardeners in their locality.

○ The single most effective policy intervention to erode class and gender inequalities may be the expansion of participation in higher education.

○ Children who are exposed to cultural experiences – visiting museums, galleries, the theatre – are more likely to build up their cultural capital in later life. Youngsters who take part in volunteering programmes at school are far more likely to continue volunteering later in life. Programmes such as Creative Partnerships, which exposes young children to creative learning, should be expanded and volunteering should become as much a part of mainstream education as science or history. Schools should play an active role in encouraging their students' Pro-Am activities.

○ The DfES, DCMS and DTI should jointly organise a national programme aimed at 16–21-year-olds who want to spend a year pursuing social Pro-Am activities.

○ Policies to promote female Pro-Ams could include creating more informal home-based networks of women based on book groups or informal parenting support; building on the Pro-Am organisations such as the WRVS, the Women's Institute and activities in which women are already well represented, such as gardening and local volunteering.

○ Companies should introduce Pro-Am days for employees to engage in activities and volunteering.

○ One bank holiday a year could be designated as a national volunteering day, an opportunity for everyone to showcase their talents and recruit others to their cause.

○ Localised versions of the Friendster social networking website could help people to link up with others with similar interests in their neighbourhoods.

○ Pro-Ams should play a much larger role in innovation policy. Lead users should play a larger role in foresight exercises to chart the future course of innovation, and policies to deregulate markets should also open up spaces for Pro-Am innovations. Pro-Am communities are the new R & D labs of the digital economy.

○ As underused publicly-owned bandwidth is auctioned off some spectra should be reserved as an innovation

commons for techie Pro-Ams – the kind that helped
create the WiFi revolution – to play and experiment with.

O   Government should develop innovation policies to fund
open source communities as competitors to proprietary
incumbents.

O   Helping people to prepare for life beyond employment by
encouraging them to take up voluntary and Pro-Am
activities in their 40s could become a key policy to help
sustain people through a long period after the end of their
first formal career.

It was a wonderful, joyful experience. Really fascinating. It was the most pleasurable learning experience I have ever had. Very different from all previous learning I had done. And because I was enjoying it so much I retained far more of the information. It's intellectually stimulating, personally very stimulating.

Dilip Lakhani, Pro-Am garden designer

The place where I feel most comfortable is on the mountain. It's very simple it's you and the mountain. It's cities that make things confusing and complex. There is no challenge that I've been up for that I did not know how to handle. It is very simple it's all down to you and if you cannot do it there is no one else to blame.

Brendan Sheehan, Pro-Am mountain climber

They are professionals who are becoming amateurs to continue to do what they love doing. Amateurs do things for the love of it. And the advantage of doing something for the love of it is that it does not become a job. As a result, it stays more loveable. You do not have an agent to boss you around and you do not have to take parts you don't really want because it's your only source of income. As an amateur you have more choice about what you do. You only have to do what you love doing.

Alison Maguire, Pro-Am actor

8. The future of Pro-Ams

Karl Marx was perhaps the original prophet of the Pro-Am economy. In *The German Ideology*, written between 1845 and 1847, Marx maintained that labour – forced, unspontaneous and waged work – would be superseded by self-activity. He evoked a communist society in which: '. . . nobody has one exclusive sphere of activity but each can become accomplished in any branch he wishes . . . to hunt in the morning, fish in the afternoon, rear cattle in the evening, criticize after dinner, just as I have a mind without ever becoming hunter, fisherman, shepherd or critic.'[49] By the mid-1850s Marx had already modified this utopian vision and instead looked forward to a time when 'material production leaves every person surplus time for other activities'.

That vision is slowly coming to fruition, at least for the share of the population of the developed world with Pro-Am passions and the means to pursue them. At some point in an extended lifespan, which will have many more stages, twists and turns, they will be able to engage in 'self-activity': a labour they love. At one level, Pro-Am culture is just a lifestyle choice over which hobbies to engage in: DIY and gardening, homes and leisure, men in sheds wearing anoraks. Yet in another sense the development of Pro-Am culture has great social significance. As more people have more time, money and inclination to find their own distinctive definition of self-fulfilment they will turn to Pro-Am activities. As more people make that move, it will set off other shifts in society.

Knowledge, once held tightly in the hands of professionals and their institutions, will start to flow into networks of dedicated amateurs. The crude, all or nothing, categories we use to carve up society – leisure versus work, professional versus amateur – will need to be rethought. The Pro-Ams will bring new forms of organisation into life, which are collaborative, networked, light on structure and largely self-regulating.

Professionals – in science and medicine, war and politics, education and welfare – shaped the twentieth century through their knowledge, authority and institutions. They will still be vital in the twenty-first century. But the new driving force, creating new streams of knowledge, new kinds of organisations, new sources of authority, will be the Pro-Ams.

Notes

1   N Klein, *No Logo* (London: Flamingo, 2000); N Hertz, *Silent Takeover: global capitalism and the death of democracy* (London: William Heinemann, 2001).

2   I Tuomi, *Networks of Innovation* (Oxford: Oxford University Press, 2001).

3   For an account of a Pro-Am culture that preceded and paved the way for the internet, see D Gregory and P Share, *Hello World: a life in ham radio* (New York: Princeton Architectural Press, 2003).

4   P Himanen, *The Hacker Ethic* (London: Secker and Warburg, 2001).

5   P Miller, 'The rise of network campaigning', in H McCarthy, P Miller and P Skidmore (eds), *Network Logic: who governs in an interconnected world?* (London: Demos, 2004).

6   JC Herz, *Gaming and the Art of Innovation* (Amsterdam: Doors of Perception Conference, Nov 2002); available at: www.doorsofperception.com

7   For an account of Grameen's growth and other social entrepreneurs, see David Bornstein, *How to Change the World* (Oxford: Oxford University Press, 2004).

8   L Allison, *Amateurism in Sport* (London: Cass, 2001); A Smith and D Porter, *Amateurs and Professionals in Post-War British Sport* (London: Cass, 2000).

9   T Ferris, *Seeing in the Dark* (London: Simon and Schuster, 2002).

10 UT is Universal Time, the standard astronomers use, the equivalent of Greenwich Meantime.

11 T Ferris, *Seeing in the Dark.*

12 See www.space.com/scienceastronomy/astronomy/dobson_astronomer_000507.html

13 J Lankford, in *Sky & Telescope*, November 1988.

14 One of the few books to explore the nature of amateurism and professionalism is R Stebbins, *Amateurs, Professionals and Serious Leisure* (Montreal: McGill-Queens University Press, 1992).

15 R Abrams, *The Playful Self* (London: Fourth Estate, 1997).

16 R Putnam, *Bowling Alone* (London: Simon and Schuster, 2000).

17 See www.pewinternet.org

18   Cited in *Promoting Sport in The Community* (HM Treasury Publication, Nov 2001).

19   P Bourdieu, *Distinction: a social critique of the judgement of taste* (London: RKP, 1985).

20   J Gershuny, *A New Measure of Social Position: social mobility and human capital in Britain* (Colchester: Institute for Social and Economic Research (ISER), University of Essex, Working Paper 2002-2).

21   J Rifkin, *The Age of Access* (London: Penguin, 2002).

22   G Privette, 'Peak Experience, Peak Performance and Peak Flow', *Journal of Personality and Social Psychology* 45 (1983).

23   M Argyle, *The Psychology of Happiness* (London: Routledge, 1989).

24   N Donovan and D Halpern, *Life Satisfaction: the state of knowledge and implications for government* (London: UK Government Strategy Unit, December 2002).

25   See P Kane, *The Play Ethic: a manifesto for a new way of living* (London: Macmillan, 2004).

26   M Savage, *Class Analysis and Social Transformation* (Buckingham: Open University Press, 2000).

27   *Curiosity Culture*, Discovery Channel, 2000.

28   H Rheingold, *Smart Mobs: the next social revolution* (New York: Perseus, 2003).

29   I Beckett, *The Amateur Military Tradition* (Manchester: Manchester University Press, 1991).

30   Ibid.

31   Putnam, *Bowling Alone*.

32   Rheingold, *Smart Mobs*.

33   J Uglow, *The Lunar Men* (London: Faber and Faber, 2002).

34   E von Hippel, *The Sources of Innovation* (Oxford: Oxford University Press, 1988).

35   See S Shah, 'From innovation to firm formation in the windsurfing, skateboarding, and snowboarding industries', University of Illinois at Urbana-Champaign; available at: http://mba.tuck.dartmouth.edu/pages/faculty/andrew.king/Papers/Sonali%20Shah%20-%202004-08-02.pdf

36   B Nooteboom, *Learning and Innovation in Organisations and Economies* (Oxford: Oxford University Press, 2000).

37   Miller, 'The rise of network campaigning' in McCarthy et al, *Network Logic*.

38   FJ Dyson, 'In Praise of Amateurs', *The New York Review of Books* XLIX, no 19 (5 Dec 2002).

39   Source: Future Foundation, nVision Service, 2004 (www.futurefoundation.net).

40   Perri 6, 'Your friendship networks' in McCarthy et al, *Network Logic*.

41   Source: Future Foundation, nVision Service, 2004. See for example M Castells, *The Power of Identity* (Oxford: Blackwells, 1997).

42   Details of the scheme and its US counterpart are available at www.bbc.co.uk/gardening.

43   R Inglehart and P Norris, *Rising Tide: gender equality and culture change around the world* (Cambridge: Cambridge University Press, 2003).

44   K Robson, *Teenage Time Use as Investment in Cultural Capital* (Colchester: ISER, University of Essex, Working Paper 2003-12).

45   The Electoral Commission, *Gender and Political Participation* (London: The Electoral Commission Research Report, April 2004).

46   Abrams, *The Playful Self*.

47   SP Jenkins and L Osberg, *Nobody to Play With? The Implications of Leisure Coordination* (Colchester: ISER, University of Essex, Working Paper 2003-19).

48   See www.friendster.com

49   K Marx, *The German Ideology* (London: Lawrence and Wishart, 1942).

DEMOS – Licence to Publish

1. **Definitions**
   a **"Collective Work"** means a work, such as a periodical issue, anthology or encyclopedia, in which the Work in its entirety in unmodified form, along with a number of other contributions, constituting separate and independent works in themselves, are assembled into a collective whole. A work that constitutes a Collective Work will not be considered a Derivative Work (as defined below) for the purposes of this Licence.
   b **"Derivative Work"** means a work based upon the Work or upon the Work and other pre-existing works, such as a musical arrangement, dramatization, fictionalization, motion picture version, sound recording, art reproduction, abridgment, condensation, or any other form in which the Work may be recast, transformed, or adapted, except that a work that constitutes a Collective Work or a translation from English into another language will not be considered a Derivative Work for the purpose of this Licence.
   c **"Licensor"** means the individual or entity that offers the Work under the terms of this Licence.
   d **"Original Author"** means the individual or entity who created the Work.
   e **"Work"** means the copyrightable work of authorship offered under the terms of this Licence.
   f **"You"** means an individual or entity exercising rights under this Licence who has not previously violated the terms of this Licence with respect to the Work, or who has received express permission from DEMOS to exercise rights under this Licence despite a previous violation.
2. **Fair Use Rights.** Nothing in this licence is intended to reduce, limit, or restrict any rights arising from fair use, first sale or other limitations on the exclusive rights of the copyright owner under copyright law or other applicable laws.
3. **Licence Grant.** Subject to the terms and conditions of this Licence, Licensor hereby grants You a worldwide, royalty-free, non-exclusive, perpetual (for the duration of the applicable copyright) licence to exercise the rights in the Work as stated below:
   a to reproduce the Work, to incorporate the Work into one or more Collective Works, and to reproduce the Work as incorporated in the Collective Works;
   b to distribute copies or phonorecords of, display publicly, perform publicly, and perform publicly by means of a digital audio transmission the Work including as incorporated in Collective Works;
   The above rights may be exercised in all media and formats whether now known or hereafter devised. The above rights include the right to make such modifications as are technically necessary to exercise the rights in other media and formats. All rights not expressly granted by Licensor are hereby reserved.
4. **Restrictions.** The licence granted in Section 3 above is expressly made subject to and limited by the following restrictions:
   a You may distribute, publicly display, publicly perform, or publicly digitally perform the Work only under the terms of this Licence, and You must include a copy of, or the Uniform Resource Identifier for, this Licence with every copy or phonorecord of the Work You distribute, publicly display, publicly perform, or publicly digitally perform. You may not offer or impose any terms on the Work that alter or restrict the terms of this Licence or the recipients' exercise of the rights granted hereunder. You may not sublicence the Work. You must keep intact all notices that refer to this Licence and to the disclaimer of warranties. You may not distribute, publicly display, publicly perform, or publicly digitally perform the Work with any technological measures that control access or use of the Work in a manner inconsistent with the terms of this Licence Agreement. The above applies to the Work as incorporated in a Collective Work, but this does not require the Collective Work apart from the Work itself to be made subject to the terms of this Licence. If You create a Collective Work, upon notice from any Licencor You must, to the extent practicable, remove from the Collective Work any reference to such Licensor or the Original Author, as requested.
   b You may not exercise any of the rights granted to You in Section 3 above in any manner that is primarily intended for or directed toward commercial advantage or private monetary

compensation. The exchange of the Work for other copyrighted works by means of digital file-sharing or otherwise shall not be considered to be intended for or directed toward commercial advantage or private monetary compensation, provided there is no payment of any monetary compensation in connection with the exchange of copyrighted works.

c   If you distribute, publicly display, publicly perform, or publicly digitally perform the Work or any Collective Works, You must keep intact all copyright notices for the Work and give the Original Author credit reasonable to the medium or means You are utilizing by conveying the name (or pseudonym if applicable) of the Original Author if supplied; the title of the Work if supplied. Such credit may be implemented in any reasonable manner; provided, however, that in the case of a Collective Work, at a minimum such credit will appear where any other comparable authorship credit appears and in a manner at least as prominent as such other comparable authorship credit.

5. Representations, Warranties and Disclaimer

a   By offering the Work for public release under this Licence, Licensor represents and warrants that, to the best of Licensor's knowledge after reasonable inquiry:

  i   Licensor has secured all rights in the Work necessary to grant the licence rights hereunder and to permit the lawful exercise of the rights granted hereunder without You having any obligation to pay any royalties, compulsory licence fees, residuals or any other payments;

  ii   The Work does not infringe the copyright, trademark, publicity rights, common law rights or any other right of any third party or constitute defamation, invasion of privacy or other tortious injury to any third party.

b   EXCEPT AS EXPRESSLY STATED IN THIS LICENCE OR OTHERWISE AGREED IN WRITING OR REQUIRED BY APPLICABLE LAW, THE WORK IS LICENCED ON AN "AS IS" BASIS, WITHOUT WARRANTIES OF ANY KIND, EITHER EXPRESS OR IMPLIED INCLUDING, WITHOUT LIMITATION, ANY WARRANTIES REGARDING THE CONTENTS OR ACCURACY OF THE WORK.

6. Limitation on Liability. EXCEPT TO THE EXTENT REQUIRED BY APPLICABLE LAW, AND EXCEPT FOR DAMAGES ARISING FROM LIABILITY TO A THIRD PARTY RESULTING FROM BREACH OF THE WARRANTIES IN SECTION 5, IN NO EVENT WILL LICENSOR BE LIABLE TO YOU ON ANY LEGAL THEORY FOR ANY SPECIAL, INCIDENTAL, CONSEQUENTIAL, PUNITIVE OR EXEMPLARY DAMAGES ARISING OUT OF THIS LICENCE OR THE USE OF THE WORK, EVEN IF LICENSOR HAS BEEN ADVISED OF THE POSSIBILITY OF SUCH DAMAGES.

7. Termination

a   This Licence and the rights granted hereunder will terminate automatically upon any breach by You of the terms of this Licence. Individuals or entities who have received Collective Works from You under this Licence, however, will not have their licences terminated provided such individuals or entities remain in full compliance with those licences. Sections 1, 2, 5, 6, 7, and 8 will survive any termination of this Licence.

b   Subject to the above terms and conditions, the licence granted here is perpetual (for the duration of the applicable copyright in the Work). Notwithstanding the above, Licensor reserves the right to release the Work under different licence terms or to stop distributing the Work at any time; provided, however that any such election will not serve to withdraw this Licence (or any other licence that has been, or is required to be, granted under the terms of this Licence), and this Licence will continue in full force and effect unless terminated as stated above.

8. Miscellaneous

a   Each time You distribute or publicly digitally perform the Work or a Collective Work, DEMOS offers to the recipient a licence to the Work on the same terms and conditions as the licence granted to You under this Licence.

b   If any provision of this Licence is invalid or unenforceable under applicable law, it shall not affect the validity or enforceability of the remainder of the terms of this Licence, and without further action by the parties to this agreement, such provision shall be reformed to the minimum extent necessary to make such provision valid and enforceable.

c   No term or provision of this Licence shall be deemed waived and no breach consented to unless such waiver or consent shall be in writing and signed by the party to be charged with such waiver or consent.

d   This Licence constitutes the entire agreement between the parties with respect to the Work licensed here. There are no understandings, agreements or representations with respect to the Work not specified here. Licensor shall not be bound by any additional provisions that may appear in any communication from You. This Licence may not be modified without the mutual written agreement of DEMOS and You.